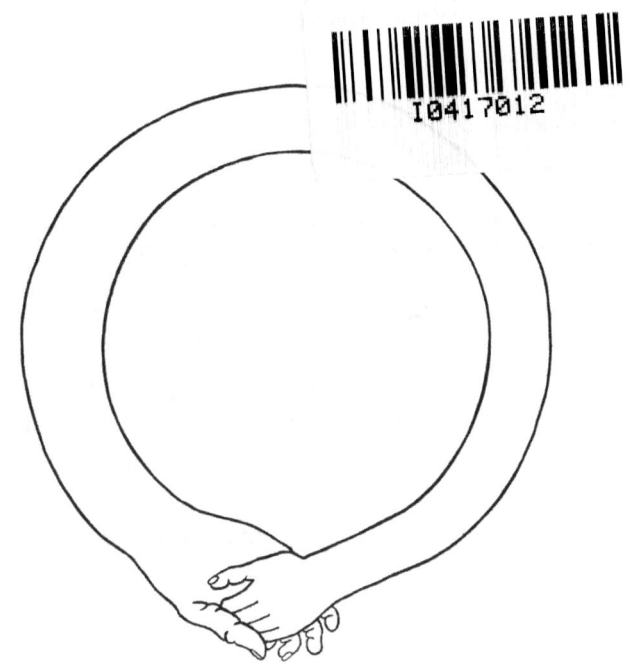

# Perry Thinks

## About Changing Negative to Positive

*Written and Illustrated by*
**Suzy Chase-Motzkin**

ur Life Skills

New York

---

*The illustrations are left without color, so readers can express themselves creatively and become more invested in the story. Colored pencils work the best.*

Text Copyright ©2011 by Suzy Chase-Motzkin
Illustrations Copyright ©2011 by Suzy Chase-Motzkin
All rights reserved.
Revised 2015 Second Printing

#4 in the Our Life Skills Series

info@ourlifeskills.com
CreateSpace Independent Publishing Platform
North Charleston, SC
Printed in the United States of America

The author of this book does not presume to offer psychological therapy nor advocate the use of any technique for the treatment of any specific or traumatic psychological condition without the approval and guidance of a qualified psychologist. The intent of the author is only to relate her personal experience in the hope that it may help understanding and develop coping mechanisms. If you use any of the information as a form of self-therapy, the author and publisher assume no responsibility for your actions.

ISBN-13: 978-1511869270
ISBN-10: 1511869275
LCC #: 2015907224

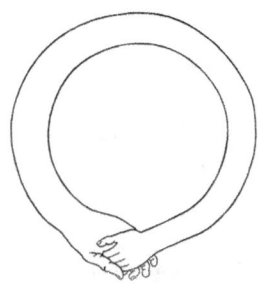

## Dedication

to Lisa and all teachers
who truly respect
young people and
encourage them to
follow their dreams and
believe in themselves

# Author's Note

Studies on consciousness go back as far as written history. Prophets, physicists, psychologists, psychiatrists, anthropologists, and neuroscientists – to name a few – have tried to understand the human psyche and the processes of the brain and its effect on the body and one's environment. Present technology enables us to map the brain and its electromagnetic emissions to determine how thought processes affect outcomes in our physical being.

More difficult to quantify, is how thoughts affect what experiences come into our lives, or how others are influenced by our thoughts. Research shows, however, that one's thoughts can influence other living things. People who have an unshakable sense of conviction that they have the goods to be successful, are often at the top of their field, whether in sports, arts, or business.

Was it because I grew up fairly free of worry with parents who reassured me? Their outlook on life was practical and they met challenges head on. When I faced conflict/contrast, they suggested I ask myself if I can change the situation. Would action make a difference for the better? Act on what you can do and avoid fretting about things that have already happened. Learn from the situation and move on, all the wiser. Change what you can and let go of the things that are unchangeable.

My father placed a significant emphasis on thinking critically. He would exercise our brains at the dinner table by having us figure out the answers to our own questions. Through our conversations, we were able to talk through various scenarios and rationally discern which tactics were best to follow. Instead of thinking we had problems, we considered the situation, instead, to be a challenge for which we can find a solution.

Even with all those thinking strategies, an important

element was missing. My sister-in-law, Lisa, taught me it. She demonstrated exactly how powerful self-talk/thinking was in accomplishing one's goals. One night at dinner she showed us an activity that would change, from that moment forward, how I raised my children and coached athletes. This activity convinced me, and all who I have shown it to, the remarkable results of switching words around to elicit a positive response or outcome. The results are undeniable, as Perry and his friends learn in this story.

People develop habits of thinking, which can be either useful or harmful to living a happy life. By practicing more positive self-talk, our health can be improved and we will often accomplish our goals because of it. When teaching or instructing others, framing those instructions positively will elicit far better outcomes.

Children constantly observe and model what they see. Family members who speak about themselves negatively as a habit will likely affect the youngsters around them. By practicing positive self-talk and thinking, we can give our children the tools to move through life successfully. Families that use positive language and practice positive thinking as a habit will find great happiness.

There is brain plasticity research indicating even people who are aging or aged, can redirect neural pathways. It is their behavior modification and self-talk that turns the switch. So, it would seem we can always continue to create a better or happier 'me'.

With Love and Positive Thoughts,
Suzy Chase-Motzkin

# Perry Thinks

Perry opened the mailbox with great anticipation. His friend, Mike, had just called to say he received the notice telling him who his sixth grade teacher was going to be.

Mike was assigned to Miss Bottalico's class, and shared with Perry, "I hear she is really nutty and she gives strange assignments to the class. There are all kinds of rumors. I wish I had Mr. Morgan. I hear he never gives homework. "

Perry did not know what to think. He had also heard the rumors.

Among the mail, Perry spotted the school logo on an envelope. He excitedly ran inside to tell his mother. It was not a teacher he was hoping for - any one other than Miss Bottalico. During the previous weeks he had said to himself, over and over, "I don't want Miss Bottalico!"

Perry's mouth dropped open when he read the words. Mommy just smiled and told him she was sure he would make the most of the situation.

Perry jumped on his bike and rode to Mike's house to share the news. On the way over, he passed his neighbor, Allie, who was just getting into her mother's car.

She called out, stopping Perry, "Hey, Perry! What teacher do you have this year? I have Miss Bottalico."

"Me, too. It will be a new adventure, I guess," answered Perry.

"We are in the same class! My mom takes yoga with her and thinks she will be a great teacher for us," said Allie as she entered the car.

Perry choked out, "I hope so," as he started to peddle his bike away down the lane.

On the first day of school, all the kids were scattered around the classroom loudly talking with each other when the bell rang to begin school. Instead of yelling out to the class to take their seats, Miss Bottalico softly said they could finish their conversations.

When they were ready, they could quietly sit in their chairs to begin class. She smiled and sat at her desk with her hands folded.

It got louder for a moment, then the kids gradually quieted and found their seats. Miss Bottalico began with, "Good morning everyone, welcome to the sixth grade!

You may have noticed that I allowed you finish your conversations. I did so, because it is respectful and I am sure you will be just as respectful to me.

You may call me, Miss B, and we will work and learn together. I look forward to learning from you, too."

Late in the day, the class was instructed to write down the question, 'What do I want to be when I grow up and how will I make it happen?' The class was told to write a three-paragraph essay, as she had illustrated on the board.

Perry was flabbergasted there was any homework on the first day of school. Miss B was on a mission.

"I would like you to do the essay in a certain order. Today, you will sit quietly for five minutes with your eyes closed and only pay attention to your breathing.

Immediately after, spend at least fifteen minutes writing your outline. Think about it for a while, and then tomorrow, add to the outline.

Wednesday, you will begin writing the paper. Thursday, you will look it over and edit. On Friday you will bring it to school.

Any questions?" she said as the bell rang, ending the school day.

On the bus, Allie plopped herself in the seat next to Perry. She groaned, "Miss B is pretty peculiar; smiling all the time like she knew a secret.

My mom started doing this inner smile thing when she gets frazzled. She learned it at that yoga class with Miss B. I am trying to understand why she wants us to sit with our eyes closed before writing."

Perry pondered, "I guess it is like meditating to clear the mind or something. Do you have any idea what you want to be or do?"

"I have it all figured out. I am going to be a famous actress," she boasted.

"A famous one? I've never seen you in any school plays," Perry smiled.

Allie giggled, "Good things take time and I'm working on it. How about you?"

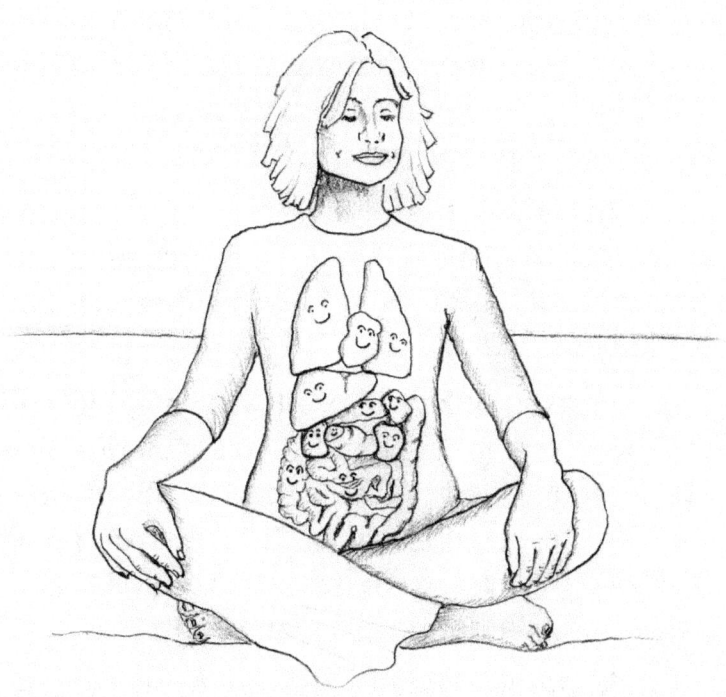

Perry settled in the seat and fixed his eyes on the scenery they were driving by. He sighed to Allie, "I have not decided."

He did not have to say much more. Allie went on and on about the plays she was thinking of doing and the part of the city she would move to one day.

Perry's mother was waiting for him in the kitchen with a snack when he returned home. She excitedly asked him how his first day had turned out.

Perry plunked himself at the table and put his head in his hands, "We got our first assignment today. We have to write about what we want to be and how we think we are going to make it happen. Geeze, I am only in sixth grade and I do not have a plan yet."

Mommy kissed his forehead saying, "I am sure you will come up with something interesting."

As it turned out, Perry actually enjoyed writing his paper. He decided that being a doctor would be interesting when he was looking at surgery images on the Internet. He imagined himself in an operating room working with robotic tools. He thought about how he was going to accomplish a goal like that.

In his research, he found there would be a lot of studying, followed by a lot of testing. He wrote that he was not sure if he could do the testing part, because he often switched numbers and letters when reading.

The following Monday, Miss B held the stack of essays in her hand as she addressed the class.

"I was so impressed by all of the things you want to do when you grow up. You all did a great job on the 'what' and the 'why' part of the essay.

Almost every one of you had difficulty with the 'how' part of the essay. Everyone wrote of problems, rather than solutions, to accomplishing their goals. And every one, used negative language at one point or another."

The kids looked puzzled as she continued.

"For instance," Miss B read off of the papers, "'If I don't fail my exams, I might be able to get into the right school', and 'I want to be a professional basketball player, but I am not tall enough', and 'I want to own a company, but that takes a lot of money.' The only exception was someone who wrote, 'I will go to every audition until I get hired'."

Perry looked immediately to Allie, who triumphantly smiled.

"Allie, will you please come up to the front of the class? You, too, Mike," Miss B said.

They looked around the class and shrugged their shoulders. Mike stood like a giant next to Allie.

Mike puffed up his chest and flexed his muscles when Miss B questioned, "Would you all agree that Mike might be a bit stronger than Allie?"

The class laughed in agreement.

"Mike, you are going to hold your arm out to the side and Allie is going to try to pull it down. While holding your arm out, say three times, 'I will hold my arm up'. "

Mike raised his arm and repeated the words 'I will hold my arm up'. Try as she might, Allie could not pull down Mike's arm.

Miss B instructed Mike to change the words to 'don't drop my arm.' Holding his arm out, Mike repeated 'don't drop my arm' three times. Allie pulled his arm and it flopped to his side. Everyone laughed.

"Wait a minute! I wasn't ready!" protested Mike. "Let me try it again!"

"Of course, you can try it again," Miss B agreed.

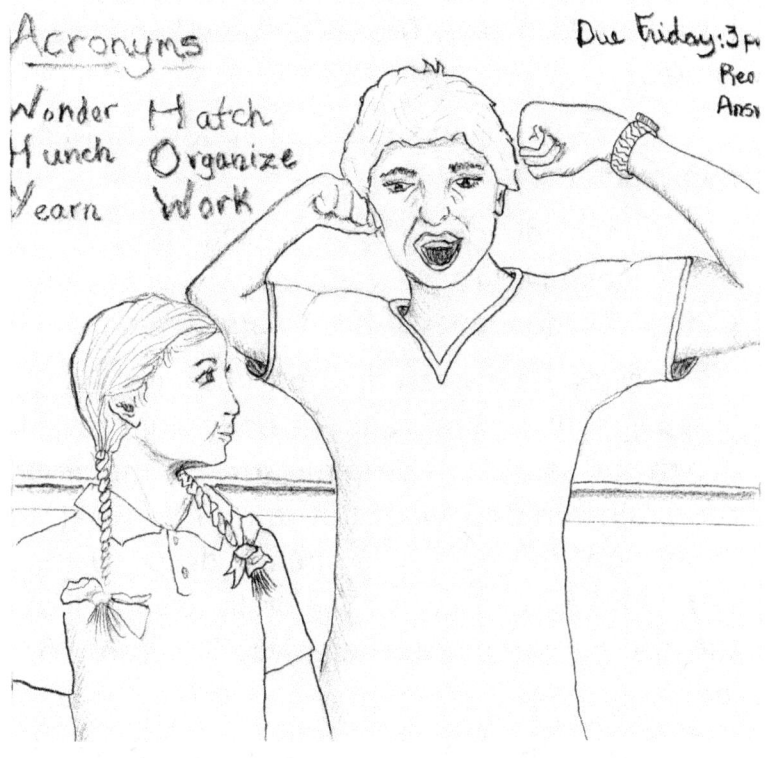

Again, he repeated, 'don't drop my arm', and again, Allie easily pulled his arm down. Miss B suggested he change the words back to 'hold my arm up'. When he repeated those words, his arm held strong. The class buzzed and Mike smiled.

"Everyone, find a partner and try it," Miss B instructed.

Soon, everyone experienced the power of the language. There was a lot of laughter and protest. Some argued it had to be a trick.

Miss B answered, "Your thoughts and language tell the brain and the body what to do. When you say, 'don't drop my arm', by the time the brain converts what not to do into what it should do, the body has already dropped the arm. It takes too long for the brain to sort all of the options when using negatives like, 'can't' or 'don't'.

Your next assignment is to observe others. List examples of their uses of negative language when giving instructions, or speaking of themselves."

Perry's parents gave him nothing to write down. In fact, it was like they had heard the assignment and purposely avoided the use of negatives.

His father came close. When Perry reached across the table, he said excitedly, "Watch your glass of milk!"

Perry realized that it was positive, even though it was louder than normal. It reminded him of a time when he was younger at his Grandma's house.

She had called out, 'Don't spill your milk!' Within moments, it was splashed across the table. Perry began to understand why he might have knocked it over. His grandma should have said, "Keep the glass of milk upright."

Perry, who was mostly happy and successful, found it interesting that his parents were mostly positive and encouraging. He thought, however, of his troubled friend who's parents always pointed out problems and called him 'bad'.

The following day in gym class, while playing basketball, the teacher gave Perry plenty of examples. The teacher yelled, 'Don't throw the ball that way!', 'You can't travel with the ball!' and 'Don't crowd the ball'.

Not once did he say anything positive to the class. Though Perry had tried to do a better job, he just kept on getting worse.

Then, after school during soccer practice, the coach did the same thing. He kept telling the team what they were doing wrong. Then, he would add a reinforcing statement like, 'Don't touch that ball with your hands!' when they started to play.

Perry kept on thinking about what not to do, instead of what he should do. This made him play poorly.

He realized, when he switched the words around in his head to a positive statement, he improved. He started to see how thought and language affected his performance.

When Perry returned home, their neighbor was talking with his mother. She loved to talk and was going on and on about her latest surgery. She even lifted her shirt to reveal the bandage on her belly. She moaned about having so many problems with her health.

Perry noticed, that as long as he could remember, she rarely said something was good. She only spoke of suffering. She would say something like; 'I hope I don't get an infection in the hospital', and it would happen. Or, 'I know I'm going to get the flu that is going around', and then, she would get ill.

Thinking about his neighbor reminded him about his friend, who always complained about not doing well in school. He would say, 'I'm terrible at taking tests'. Even though he would study and know the material, his grades were usually bad.

At school, Miss B asked the students about their observations, "Who would like to share some examples?"

A boy shared a story about being in the car with his parents, "Mom was driving and Dad said, 'Don't turn into that lane.' Just after he said it, she turned into the lane anyway. Dad whined that Mom never listens to him.

So, I told them about the arm thing we did in class and they thought it was neat. Dad said he would try to say something like, 'stay in this lane' in the future."

"That is a great example," replied Miss B.

Another boy raised his hand, "My bus driver yelled, 'don't stand up while the bus is moving!' He has to say it almost every day. Maybe if he said, 'sit down while the bus is moving', he wouldn't have to say it all the time."

She agreed and called upon Perry next.

"Yesterday the Phys Ed. teacher and our soccer coach kept on using negatives. They both said 'don't this or that', and when they said something positive, it was about what we were doing wrong.

Last summer at soccer camp, the coaches, who were professional athletes, only told us how to do things better. When they pointed out our mistakes, they always followed with ways to improve our performance.

One of the athletes gave a talk about how he made it to the Olympics. He said that success depends upon a lot of hard work and a positive attitude. Now, I really understand what he was talking about," Perry shared.

"Yes, Perry, how we choose to speak or think can make all the difference in the world. By being aware of our thinking, we can change negatives into positives. When we do that, we can change our lives for the better."

Miss B pointed to Allie who had been waving her hand excitedly.

Allie responded, "You sound just like my mother. She always tells me I can do or be anything I put my mind to. She always makes me change, 'I can't' to 'I can', or 'I will try'. Sometimes it is really hard to do."

"Yes, Allie, it takes a lot of self discipline to get started, but after a while it will come naturally."

A boy in the back of the class hesitantly raised his hand. Miss B called upon him before he could put it down, "Whenever my dad gets a new job, he always complains about his boss not being fair, or they never appreciate how hard he works. He can't seem to keep a job longer than a few months. How can I help him be more positive?"

Miss B answered thoughtfully, "There is not much we can do to change other people. We can only change how we think and speak. Hopefully, others will learn by our example.

Maybe if you appreciate him, he will feel better about himself. When we believe in ourselves and our capabilities, others also start to believe."

"My mother always says what we fear the most is attracted to us, like a magnet attracts metal, because we worry about it too much. She says, it is better to focus our attention on what we want, instead of what we don't want," Allie added.

Perry excitedly interrupted, "Yes, like our neighbor, who is always talking about having problems with her health. It seems that she is always getting sick.

When I broke my arm, I thought really hard about it healing quickly. It did; way faster than anyone thought possible."

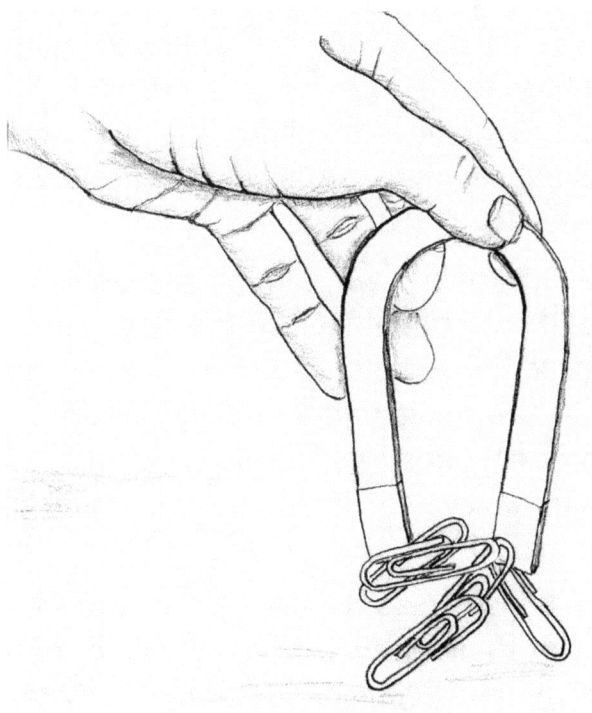

"Allie, I believe your mom is right, and Perry, people get into habits. Some people chew on pencils, or are always late to appointments. There can be habits of thinking, too; like being angry, impatient, or worried. I have noticed that people, who dwell on the negative things in their lives, seem to attract more negative things.

Like any habit, we can train ourselves to change. It may be difficult in the beginning, but with practice and attention, our choices in language or action, can affect positive change. We are the only ones responsible for choosing what to think or say – to ourselves and to others. We all can make being positive a habit!"

Miss B instructed the class to rewrite the 'How' part of their essay. Everyone was to find the negatives and change them to positives. She told the class she was hoping they would remember this assignment as they continued on their life journeys.

Perry certainly did.

The End

# About the Author

As a coach and parent, who also collaborated with 'at-risk' students in writing and performing numerous inspirational original plays, Suzy Chase-Motzkin understands the need for helping children and their families learn how to reframe thinking and cope with the challenges they are facing.

Suzy is deeply committed to the research of human development, consciousness, motivation, the use of language, and the power of the mind regarding performance and healing.

Discovering many effective modalities, she put into practice the concepts while raising her own children and coaching others. Her methodologies proved to be very powerful in elevating self-esteem, reducing stress, and helping children (and many adults) realize their potential.

Suzy was inspired to write stories that would teach people life skills by engaging the reader and imparting conventional wisdom surreptitiously. In an effort to hold the young reader's attention, she committed to making an illustration for each page of text.

Her mother, a prolific artist who held a Master of Fine Art, encouraged Suzy to illustrate the stories herself. With her mother cheering her on, Suzy grabbed a pencil and paper and began. Initially, so much time was spent erasing lines to get the perspective right that she switched to using a graphics program on the computer, where fixing her mistakes was far less time consuming.

When not coaching or creating, Suzy continues to share her gifts as a healer, teacher, and writer by presenting seminars nationally and internationally. She can be contacted at: www.OurLifeSkills.com

# About the Series

The Our Life Skills Perry stories are designed to teach readers life skills through the telling of a story. Perry, his parents, and friends discover ways of thinking, seeing, and being that embellishes their lives. Each story inspires the readers with ideas about how to live life with reduced conflict and stress while elevating their ability to communicate effectively, sleep better, modify or re-frame thinking, cope with situations pragmatically, and visualize positive outcomes. The reader is left with profound insights and cognitive tools to ensure a lifelong ability to look at people and situations through the lens of love, compassion, respect, and understanding.

## Perry's Star
*About Meditation for Sleep or Anxiety*

## Perry Heals
*About Imagery and Self-Healing*

## Perry Sees
*About Awareness and Intuition*

## Perry Thinks
*About Changing Negative to Positive*

## Perry's Friends
*About Character and Understanding*

www.OurLifeSkills.com

www.ingramcontent.com/pod-product-compliance
Lightning Source LLC
Chambersburg PA
CBHW071014290526
45795CB00005B/1795